I0621057

Divinely Blessed

How To Achieve Limitless Abundance and Fulfill God's Purpose For Your Life

CRYSTAL DAYE

ISBN: **978-1-958443-93-4 (paperback)**
        978-1-958443-94-1 (hardback)

Acknowledgments

I am super grateful for the opportunity to walk in my purpose and calling – to inspire women of all ages to become the best God has called them to be. It is a divine assignment that I don't take lightly, and I am so humbled that God chose me to do this work.

Thank You, Lord, for all the blessings, lessons, and breakthroughs.

Thank you to my family for their love and continuous support.

Thanks to the DayeLight Publishers team for helping to bring this book to life.

Thanks to my community (readers, clients, social media family) for allowing me to serve you with my gifts.

Endorsements

Divinely Blessed packs a powerful message that will empower anyone interested in unblocking blessings, attracting abundance, and living a more fulfilling life. It is a remedy for limiting beliefs and an encouraging reminder that prosperity is possible regardless of your past or current circumstances. The success strategies offered are practical, motivational, and rooted in Godly principles. No matter where you are in life, reading this book will inspire you to rise higher and draw closer to who God created you to be. Divinely Blessed is a spirit-lifting read and a catalyst for meaningful and lasting transformation.

Andromeda
Founder of She Wins Society

Crystal Daye delivers a life-changing guide that every individual who knows they are "called and made for more than they are currently settling for" needs. Divinely Blessed masterfully combines faith, strategy, and purpose to empower individuals to unlock their God-given potential and live in the limitless abundance God desires. From aligning your mindset with heaven's principles to taking bold action in your goals, this book is a practical blueprint for anyone ready to embrace the life God intended. Each of the 16 strategies is a spiritual and practical gem, offering wisdom and encouragement to propel you into divine success. Crystal's heartfelt passion and authenticity shine through every page, inspiring readers to dream big and act boldly. This is more than a book—it's a divine mandate for those ready to walk in limitless abundance and fulfill God's purpose for their lives.

Stephanie Outten
Literary Doula®
CEO of Cocoon to Wings Publishing

In a world where scarcity and fear hold people back, this book is a refreshing, faith-filled guide to claiming the abundant life God designed for you. With powerful biblical insights, practical strategies, and heartfelt honesty, the author shares a message that resonates deeply with anyone longing for more—not just material wealth but a life of purpose, impact, and joy. If you're ready to break free from limiting mindsets and step into your God-given destiny, this book will inspire and equip you.

Susan Neal
RN, MBA, MHS
Award-Winning Author of 12 Ways to Age Gracefully

This book is insightful, engaging, and a must-read for anyone interested in breaking the limits of their life to fulfill God's will. Captivating stories and strategies that will keep you turning pages until the very end. This is the definitive guide on being Divinely Blessed, irrespective of the negative thoughts that try to keep us in one position or cycle, written with clarity and authority. A powerful and thought-provoking exploration of How to achieve limitless abundance and fulfill God's purpose for your life. I couldn't put it down; my mind feels lifted, shifted, and elevated—a truly unforgettable read.

Sheena Hanson
Minister, Speaker, CEO of Sheena Power Talk

Crystal Daye's *Divinely Blessed* completely transformed how I view abundance and God's purpose for my life. From the first page, I felt like Crystal was speaking directly to my heart— sharing her own struggles, victories, and the faith lessons she learned along the way. Her story is raw and real, showing that no matter where you've been or what you've done, God's plan for you is bigger than you can imagine. This book gave me practical steps to upgrade my mindset, steward my resources, and walk boldly in my calling. Crystal's words reminded me that abundance isn't just about material things; it's about living in the fullness of God's promises. She's like that wise friend who lovingly pushes you out of your comfort zone and into your purpose. Every chapter left me encouraged, equipped, and ready to take action. I laughed, I cried, and I prayed through her words—and I'm better for it. If you're ready to stop settling

vii

and start walking in the limitless life God has for you, this book will bless you beyond measure. Crystal's journey inspired me, and I know it will inspire you too.

Roscoe Robinson
International Speaker and Coach

As I delved into the best-selling book "Divinely Blessed," I felt profound gratitude for the blessings in my life and the important reminder of putting God first. It reinforced the need for developing a personal relationship with God daily. Each chapter offers practical success strategies and self-check prompts, making this book invaluable for navigating today's challenges. Crystal's personal experiences are woven throughout, illustrating that regardless of the trials we encounter, we can overcome them with God's support and live a divinely blessed life. This book is a must-have for anyone seeking guidance and inspiration to live a divinely blessed life in God.

Hillary Dunkley-Campbell
Author, Speaker, Coach

Are you ready to unlock the abundant life you deserve? Crystal Daye's Divinely Blessed: How to Achieve Limitless Abundance and Fulfill God's Purpose for Your Life is a transformative guide that will help you break free from a scarcity mindset and step boldly into abundance. Building on

viii

the profound insights of her bestseller, Dear Insecurity, this award-winning author shares inspiring personal testimonies and fills the book with practical success strategies to help you release negative habits, live intentionally, and create a lasting legacy. More than just a book, Divinely Blessed is a blueprint for action. It challenges you to elevate your mindset, embrace self-discipline, dress for your dreams, and boldly pursue your God-given purpose. Perfect for this season, it's a must-read for anyone ready to dream bigger, live better, and make a meaningful impact on the world. Don't wait—grab your copy today and start living the divinely blessed life you were created for!

Min. Donna Morris
Author, Speaker, Life Coach
"Moved to a New Mindset: Free From Limitations, Rejections, And Fears"

Preface

Firstly, let's get this out of the way: I am not a prosperity gospel minister. I don't believe everyone is called to be rich and go around declaring everyone is getting a breakthrough. For many years, I was probably closer to the extreme that the more you "suffer," the closer you are to living holy. This mindset of poverty and suffering wasn't because I was taught this in church; it was simply based on my cultural upbringing and personal experience of growing up in the inner city. It is probably in the last three years that I came into a renewed mindset that abundance really is my birthright as a daughter of the King.

Let's go back a bit.

If you haven't read my first book, *Living a Royal Reality: Discovering Your Identity, Purpose and Worth In Christ,* you probably don't know much about my story. I grew up in Kingston, Jamaica, living in violence-ridden and poverty-stricken communities where teenage pregnancy, sleeping on the ground, going to bed hungry, and promiscuity were simply a part of our reality.

While growing up, I knew I didn't have much, but that was okay because, for the most part, my siblings and I had our basic needs met. Plus, I knew my life of lack was temporary because my father drilled it in me that getting a good education was my ticket to a better life (yes, the life on the hills with a pool, seven bedrooms, and a dope career would one day be my reality).

Despite many unfortunate experiences, like being sexually molested at age nine, and my foolish choices, like doing my first abortion at age sixteen, I kept focus on being the first in my family to achieve certain accomplishments. *(Somebody say "generational curse-breaker").*

I graduated from high school as one of the top students, got my first full-time job at a bank at age sixteen, travelled for the first time at age seventeen, graduated with my Bachelor's degree from university, purchased a car and my first apartment, had a baby after university, got a good government job, gave my siblings a lot of opportunities we couldn't afford growing up, and I made my parents proud.

Listen, you couldn't tell me that I wasn't on my way to live my "best" life because I got out of the inner city and was making something of myself. But here's the interesting part: all these amazing accomplishments were not afforded to me because of my brilliance, wisdom, or even hard work. I always knew God was *blessing* me beyond what I deserved.

Yes, it was great. I worked hard. It was good to believe in myself, and was determined to make something of life. But even though I did not grow up in church or have a "relationship" with God, I knew I wasn't self-made—it was all God.

Fast forward to today, the day I surrendered to Jesus Christ and started to give over my plans and accept His purpose; what I thought was blessings then is nothing compared to who I have become in Him and the abundance I have experienced. My Christian journey wasn't perfect. I have had some really challenging seasons, but the exceedingly abundantly spoken about in Ephesians 3:20 has definitely been my portion (and it is your portion too).

So, here's why you should continue reading this book:

- Deep down you know you are called and destined for more than you are currently settling for.
- You have some dreams in your heart, and you are afraid to share them with anyone because they might think you are crazy, but your heart tells you it is possible.
- Yes, you want to accomplish wealth and acquire nice possessions, but there is a deeper desire to impact lives and leave a legacy where God gets the glory.
- You have been inspired by many big celebrities doing great exploits for God, but you want to see someone 'normal' like you grow their influence so

you can have hope that one day it will happen for you too.

- Finally, you are driven by purpose, even though sometimes you don't know exactly what that looks like. You believe Jeremiah 29:11, which says God has a good plan for your life, and at the end of this life, you want to hear, "Well done, My faithful servant!"

If none of these scenarios relate to you, then this book is probably not for you. Thanks for the support though; maybe someone comes to mind that you can give it to as a gift. But if you read those statements and felt goosebumps or even tears welling up, I got you!

This is Holy Spirit-inspired. He knows what you need to hear and which strategy or strategies shared in this book will transform your mind so you can access all God has for you. I am simply a vessel whose life also started transforming as I wrote this book and leveled up my faith to take these steps to experience immeasurable blessings, more bookings, and greater boundlessness in my life and business.

Crystal

Table of Contents

Introduction

Over the last few years, I have had the wonderful privilege of ministering, mentoring, inspiring and coaching people of all ages from all over the world. One thing I realized we all have in common is that we place limitations on ourselves based on our abilities, experiences, mistakes, background or expectations. Even though God's Word affirms that we are all called for a purpose (see Jeremiah 29:11) and to make an impact (see Matthew 5:16), the truth is, many have died who didn't walk in those promises, and many are alive, yet settling for mediocre and hopeless lives.

The late Dr. Myles Munroe said, *"The graveyard is the richest place on the surface of the earth because there you will see the books that were not published, ideas that were not harnessed, songs that were not sung, and drama pieces that were never acted."*

For many years, I was busy living my version of a "successful" life. This meant I got an education, a decent job, mortgage, etc., but it was my plan and not God's purpose. It was okay but not abundance. What God had in

17

store for me was far bigger than I could have even imagined, asked or thought of.

As you read this book, you may know deep down that you are called and made for more than you are currently settling for. This book was written to give you the strategies, tools, encouragement and keys to finally live the purposeful, impactful and abundant life God desires and destined for you.

The biggest question many ask themselves when they do believe God is calling them for more is, *"Why would God use someone like me?"* This question alone is stemmed from not being confident in your abilities even though God has equipped you for your calling (see Hebrews 13:21), not feeling deserving of being used by God even though God has declared that He sent His Son to redeem your true identity (see John 3:16), and feeling intimidated by what others may think about you even though we should live to please God not man *(see Galatians 1:10)*.

To live a life of impact, purpose or abundance, you don't have to be fearless but you need to be obedient. Believe me, we will all experience fear as we walk in faith in our calling. You simply need to take small courageous steps towards your dreams.

Your past, what people think, and your own weaknesses will try to hinder you from tapping into your potential. But remember God only needs your yes to do a new thing in you.

The fact that you picked up this book means you desire something more for your life.

In this book, I share sixteen success strategies to help you release any scarcity-mindset holding you back from experiencing your blessed and boundless life. Rooted with biblical wisdom, guided with practical tools, and inspired by personal lessons, these strategies are guaranteed to transform your mindset, which will transform your life.

Remember, when you live life purposefully, make a kingdom impact and experience abundance, you will exemplify God's power in your life while bringing Him glory.

There's something better and bigger available for you.

Let's begin!

7 Irrefutable Rules of Living A Blessed Life

The first time I read the book, *Prayer of Jabez*, I was challenged to see blessings differently. We have this mindset that we should be modest—and even cliché as believers—to say, *"I'm blessed and highly favored,"* even if we don't feel that way. It's not that we can't feel blessed when we are grateful for anything God has given us, but when I learnt that it was not selfish to desire more, and there is no limit to how much I ask God, it was liberating.

When Jabez asked God to bless him in 1 Chronicles 4:10, he was asking God to impart supernatural favor in every area of his life. This type of blessing is when you are crying out to the omnipotent (all powerful) God for His unlimited goodness. When you think about the true BLESSED life, it is looking back at those miraculous situations where you know that you know it was ONLY God.

If you truly want to break through and live the amazing life God has in store for you—the life you will have when you choose to believe in His promises—step out in faith and walk boldly in your God-given calling.

1. **Know that it is God's nature to bless.** You might not feel like you are worthy of being blessed but that is not up to you. Just like God is love (it's just who He is), He blesses us. It is not dependent on us; it is what He does (see Matthew 7:11).

2. **Unlimited blessings exist for you.** There is no limit to how God can and will bless you. He is El Shaddai (all-sufficient) (see 2 Corinthians 9:8).

3. **Blessings are far more than money or material things.** Even though God will bless us with wealth and riches, blessings come in all forms: health, relationships, talents, experiences, etc. (see Proverbs 10:22).

4. **Blessings are not seasonal.** Sometimes you have challenging seasons in life and you are tempted to believe you are not being "blessed," but, remember that even in those rough seasons when you can't "see or feel" the blessings of God, He is always working on your behalf (see Ezekiel 34:26).

5. **If you focus on your blessing, you will experience even more blessings.** Whatever you feed grows. If you are daily seeing and acknowledging miracles, answered prayers and favor, you will begin to access more blessings.

6. **There are blessings you will only receive when you ASK.** While God is sovereign, and He will bless each of us as He sees fit, there are blessings we forfeit if we don't ask (see James 4:2).

7. **Being blessed is part of the abundant life God destined for you.** Blessing is part of our eternal inheritance that we access through faith in Jesus Christ (see Ephesians 1:3).

Success Strategy #1

Put God First

"But seek first the kingdom of God and his righteousness, and all these things will be added to you." (Matthew 6:33 – ESV).

Power Keys

- Cultivate a personal relationship with Jesus Christ.
- When you put God first, everything else falls into place.
- Keeping God first includes spending time in prayer.
- Putting God first is living with eternity in mind.

The idea of putting God first is considered the right thing to do. As a believer, it seems like the obvious thing to start with. If you are not a Christian, you may think it is a "religious" thing.

25

Let me make it clear: I wasn't born "saved" (but of course you know that), but I did not grow up in church. I lived a worldly life. Paul would say I was the sinner of sinners (see 1 Timothy 1:15) I surrendered my life to Christ as an adult, and even then, for many years, I lived lukewarm with one foot in church and the other in the world.

I share this because I want you to truly believe me when I say that you can live a blessed, purposeful, successful and impactful life when you accept Jesus Christ as your Lord and Savior, but you need to let go of your way and choose to accept God's love, grace and mercy.

Putting God first starts with accepting that God has always loved you and desires to have a personal relationship with you. This means we will choose to pursue holiness (being set apart) and walk in righteousness (being a work in progress as we grow our faith and obey Him).

If you are already a believer, it is essential that you truly do a self-check to ensure that God is truly first in your life or there are other idols present. If you don't know what idolatry looks like, you can get a copy of my book, *Empowered For Such A Time As This*. I share more on some of the other "gods" we have in our lives.

Here are four practical ways to put God first in your life:

i. Repentance

Repentance is not a one-time act when we decide to accept the gift of salvation. It should be a daily practice of turning away from evil and turning towards God.

To repent means changing your mind, heart and attitude towards God. It is manifested as change in our actions and lifestyle.

It is not about being remorseful (sorry for committing a sin or feeling guilty because you got caught). It is living a life of hating sin and living purely for Christ (see Colossians 3:5-10).

ii. See your Father's heart

Many times, we are not taught that God is truly our Father. So many people were introduced to God as a harsh judge waiting to send them to hell for making a mistake. While God is a righteous judge, He truly desires us to experience His heart for us as a Father.

Unlike our earthly fathers, who are imperfect even if they are good fathers to us, imagine if we trust in our perfect God who is our good Father. He will protect, provide, strengthen and love us unconditionally.

It is imperative we spend time in the Word of God, learning about the attributes and character of God so we can have a proper perspective of who He is to us.

One of the major reasons to start learning about God's heart for us is that it will help us to accept our identity, and we will not have a limited view of how much He truly desires to bless us.

iii. Be led by the Spirit

The Holy Spirit is a part of the triune God. In John 14:15-31, Jesus stated that He had to leave this earth so the Helper would come. Many people have a limited view of the Holy Spirit, but being led by Him is so crucial to how we impact the lives of others.

It is through living by the Spirit that we will bear fruit (joy, peace, goodness, faithfulness, gentleness, kindness, patience, love and self-control), and these attributes demonstrate our pursuit of God.

The Holy Spirit gives you gifts so you can minister to others, walk out God's will, and be empowered to live a boundless life.

iv. Living For Eternity

While living on this earth, you should keep in mind that this is all temporary. One day, Jesus will come back for His people, and this is our hope because sometimes life can really knock us down. Also, with the sadness experienced by the death of loved ones, it is comforting to know that one day we will see them again.

Living for eternity is also a reality check when we get caught up in earthly success, temporary pleasures, and storing up material possessions.

The book, *Living for Eternity*, by John Bevere was one of the books that totally transformed my thoughts toward eternal living. I encourage every believer to read that book; you won't be the same.

Learn how to truly delight yourself in the Lord by spending time with Him, falling in love with Him, obeying Him and desiring to please Him.

Self-Check Prompts

Have you truly repented? How can you practice daily repentance?

_____

_____

_____

_____

_____

What are some of the activities you are engaging in that are not pushing you closer to God?

_____

_____

What are you doing now that has an eternal purpose?

How can you be intentional about putting God first in your life?

"When we put God first, all other things fall into their proper place or drop out of our lives. Our love of the Lord will govern the claims for our affection, the demands on our time, the interests we pursue, and the order of our priorities."
—Ezra Benson

Success Strategy #2

Upgrade Your Mindset

> *"Do not be conformed to this world, but be transformed by the renewal of your mind, that by testing you may discern what is the will of God, what is good and acceptable and perfect." (Romans 12:2 - NIV).*

Power Keys

- Abundance thinking comes from a place of gratitude and appreciation.
- Having a scarcity mindset means you focus on what you don't have and what you think you don't deserve.
- Your daily decisions are dictated by what you believe, which is shaped by habits and words.
- When you choose faith over doubt, it gives you boldness—this belief that you can achieve anything regardless of the obstacles you may face.

Your mindset plays an important role in how you live a life of purpose, impact, and abundance. Your mindset is simply a collection of the dominant thoughts in your life, and it can either repel BLESSINGS or attract boundless opportunities.

"Be careful what you think, because your thoughts run your life." (Proverbs 4:23 – NCV).

Personally, I know that while I have achieved a level of success on my faith journey, I had a lot of limited beliefs, mostly believing I didn't deserve more or couldn't do better. My mindset around money was rooted in scarcity based on my upbringing—growing up in poverty.

Limited In Your Beliefs

Many people have limited beliefs that hinder their success. A limited belief is a state of mind, conviction, or belief that you think is true that limits you in some way. A limited belief tends to have a negative impact on one's life by stopping them from moving forward and growing on a personal and professional level.

Examples of limiting beliefs:

— I am not_____ enough.

— I can't _____

— I don't have enough _____
to be successful.

— I don't deserve to _____
because _____

When we train our minds to think in abundance and hold unwavering faith, we gravitate towards that. We attract good things because we believe and expect good things to come.

If you cultivate an abundance mindset, you will focus on the limitless opportunities that exist.

Your decisions are dictated by what you believe. What you believe is influenced by what you focus on.

If you are not confident in your knowledge and abilities, then you will become complacent in your pursuit of purpose.

"The only person you are destined to become is the person you decide to be."
—*Ralph Waldo Emerson*

5 Ways to Upgrade Your Mindset to Receive Abundance

1. Practice positive and Godly self-talk. In the same way you used to criticize yourself, you have to

33

retrain yourself to affirm positive declarations about your life.

2. Surround yourself with people who are pursuing purpose and making a difference.
3. Learn from other people's mistakes. Study successful people in your field. Read books.
4. Practice daily gratitude. Be grateful for the past and current blessings (small or large).
5. Set goals aligning with your dreams. Make a small step toward each of your goals daily.

Self-Check Prompts

What limiting perspective or mindset have you lived with your entire life? How are you going to work through it?

_____

_____

_____

_____

_____

What would your life look like if you were fully confident in yourself and your opinions? What steps can you take to get closer to that?

_____

_____

_____

_____

_____

What were you told you "couldn't" or "shouldn't" do as a child that you think is hindering you from accepting all the blessings God has in store for you?

_____

_____

_____

_____

_____

In what area of your life do you tend to procrastinate or make excuses?

_____

_____

_____

_____

_____

"Appreciation creates a mindset of abundance. Worry creates a mindset of scarcity."
—*Gordana Biernat*

Success Strategy #3

Develop Self-Discipline

"For the moment all discipline seems painful rather than pleasant, but later it yields the peaceful fruit of righteousness to those who have been trained by it." (Hebrews 12:11 – ESV).

Power Keys

- Discipline begins with having a desire.
- A strong desire will enable "ordinary" people to do extraordinary things.
- When you increase your discipline, you position yourself for acceleration.
- Self-discipline takes practice and grows as you progress, so start small.

There is no way we can talk about success without including self-discipline. No matter how gifted you are, praying for a breakthrough, certain

37

BLESSINGS in your life can only be accessed by becoming more disciplined.

But the word *discipline* itself just sounds so hard, right?

According to yourdictionary.com, self-discipline is the ability to control and motivate yourself, stay on track, and do what is right.

"Discipline is the bridge between goals and accomplishments."
— Jim Rohn

Becoming a person of self-discipline is a lifelong process, but it must start now. Sometimes you find yourself more disciplined in one area of your life, while in another area, you are still struggling.

That's me and exercising (argh).

The truth is, every year, people all over the world set goals but often fail to accomplish them because they lack the discipline to truly pursue them.

Discipline starts with desire, but desire alone won't be enough to cultivate successful habits. Self-discipline is a key to accessing all God has in store for us.

Be honest with yourself; what are some of the areas in your life that you know you need to become more discipline in?

One of the main reasons self-discipline seems so hard is because it requires us to sacrifice temporary pleasure for permanent gain. It is easier to eat the donut now because you crave sweets than to say no because you know those additional pounds will slow you down. If we are being real, being self-disciplined is the reason many Christians can't access their inheritance.

It starts with you simply not having the discipline to read the Bible daily, and because you don't read the Bible, you don't know God's promises, and because you don't know His promises, you stay stuck in a cycle of lack and scarcity.

Hard work is a part of experiencing the next level God has for us. Abundance is a result of being diligent in your pursuit.

Self-Control Versus Self-Discipline

The fruit of the Spirit includes self-control. This means, as believers, the Holy Spirit helps us to delay gratification, especially when it leads to sin. While we want to practice self-control, we also need self-discipline to become the best God has called us to be.

I love this example:

"DECIDING TO stop eating sweets and start eating vegetables are separate psychological functions. The first

39

takes self-control. The second takes self-discipline. You can easily succeed at one and fail at the other. They aren't the same process!"
—*Dr. Julia-Marie O'Brien*

Self-control helps us stop doing something we are already doing, while self-discipline motivates us to start a new task and stay committed to it. Self-control focuses on short-term actions, whereas self-discipline is about long-term commitment. It is important to understand both because you need both to experience true success.

So, here is where it starts: taking one step daily to cultivate healthier habits, develop daily routines, overcoming overwhelm, taking small steps, and having a greater motivation than yourself.

Self-Check Prompts

What do you really want? *(Discipline starts with desire).*

_____

_____

_____

_____

_____

What are some success habits you need to start practicing daily that take you closer to accomplishing your goals?

In what area(s) are you struggling to practice self-control?

Where would a little more self-discipline have the greatest impact on your life or success?

"We all have dreams. But in order to make dreams come into reality, it takes an awful lot of determination, dedication, self-discipline, and effort."
—*Jesse Owens*

41

Success Strategy #4

Steward Your Finances

> "For to everyone who has will more be given, and he will have an abundance. But from the one who has not, even what he has will be taken away." (Matthew 25:29 - ESV).

Power Keys

- Money or success doesn't change us; it simply amplifies who we already are.
- God holds us accountable for the things He has blessed us with.
- It is not money that is evil; it is the love of money where it becomes your idol that is evil.
- When you manage your money well, God multiples it.

Let me start by defining stewardship:

"Utilizing and managing all resources God provides for the glory of God and the betterment of His creation."
—Charles Bugg

This means everything you achieve, possess, or acquire on this earth does not belong to you. You are simply a manager with conditional authority over the resources God has blessed you with.

God owns all things; all things belong to God (see Psalm 24:1).

The idea of stewardship is hard for many to accept because people spend their lives pursuing things and realize later that they truly have no control. If you can understand the principle of stewardship and accept that God BLESSES us with things so we can use them for His purpose, then you will walk in the freedom of never worrying about lack.

Stewardship is not only about money. It includes how you manage your time, use your gifts, grow in the Word of God, and even how you take care of your body.

For this success strategy, I will be focusing on how to properly steward your finances.

Now, let me put this out there: I feel more than unqualified to write this chapter because it is really over the past few years that I learnt about money and how to properly manage it. I am not making excuses, but growing up in financial

44

hardship shaped the money decisions I have made throughout my life, leaving me in debt, without savings, and struggling with emotional spending.

But thank the Lord for His grace and mercy. It is never too late to learn how to properly steward your finances, which should lead to financial abundance.

Let's Talk About Money

There are two extremes in today's culture:

1. People spend their lives chasing money and trying to build riches (sometimes in exchange for their souls).

2. In church, we don't have healthy money conversations, and there is this notion that being poor means you are closer to God.

Money is spoken about many times in the Bible, so we must get used to having healthy conversations about it and learn how to effectively steward it.

6 Scriptures About Money To Reflect On

"No one can serve two masters. Either you will hate the one and love the other, or you will be devoted to the one and despise the other. You cannot serve both God and money." *(Matthew 6:24 – NIV).*

45

"Bring the whole tithe into the storehouse, that there may be food in my house. Test me in this," says the LORD Almighty, "and see if I will not throw open the floodgates of heaven and pour out so much blessing that there will not be room enough to store it." (Malachi 3:10 – ESV).

"He who trusts in his riches will fall, but the righteous shall flourish as the green leaf." (Proverbs 11:28 – ESV).

"The generous will themselves be blessed, for they share their food with the poor." (Proverbs 22:9 – NIV).

"Dishonest money dwindles away, but whoever gathers money little by little makes it grow." (Proverbs 13:11 - NIV).

"But remember the LORD your God, for it is he who gives you the ability to produce wealth, and so confirms his covenant, which he swore to your ancestors, as it is today." (Deuteronomy 8:18 – NIV).

4 Quotes About Money to Upgrade and Challenge Us

"Most people fail to realize that money is both a test and trust from God."
—Rick Warren

"When money realizes that it is in good hands, it wants to stay and multiply in those hands."

—*Idowu Koyenikan*

"God doesn't need us to give Him our money. He owns everything. Tithing is God's way to grow Christians."
—*Adrian Rogers*

"The person who thinks the money he makes is meant mainly to increase his comforts on earth is a fool, Jesus says. Wise people know that all their money belongs to God and should be used to show that God, and not money, is their treasure, their comfort, their joy, and their security."
—*John Piper*

While abundance is not just about money, we know it has a crucial function on this earth. Money is a medium of exchange that gives purchasing power. Having money is not sinful; it is the love of money the Bible condemns because it can become an idol; anything you put in front of God is an idol.

These are some of the lessons I am learning about being a better steward of my finances:

1. **Learn to forgive yourself if you have made poor money decisions.** No matter what age you are, it is not too late to change your mindset and become better stewards of your finances. It starts with a desire to do better. Money management is a skill you can learn, so even if you are dirt poor now, things can change if you are willing to become disciplined and

47

be diligent in the process. So, shake off the guilt of not knowing better or even doing better. You can start now!

2. **Live within your means and learn to be content.** Sometimes we get ourselves into money problems because we are trying to impress others. Be faithful with your current portion.

3. **Practice being a giver.** It doesn't make sense to give if you believe you don't have enough. Giving is a biblical principle. When you give, you are opening yourself to receive more from God.

4. **Create a budget and track your spending.** This is something I have been consciously doing since 2019, and listen, it has been a blessing. When you know where your money is going, you are able to make better decisions to allocate funds.

5. **Tithe your 10% to God.** This book is not to convince you or argue with you about tithing. It is a biblical practice, and if God says it, then it is so. If you have questions about tithing, talk to a pastor, listen to YouTube sermons, read books on the subject or simply go talk to God.

6. **Pay your bills and taxes (cover eyes).** This is about honoring your obligations and commitments. Jesus says give to Caesar what belongs to him (see

Matthew 22:21). It is not my place to decide who deserves what. It is my duty to obey God.

7. **SAVE no matter how small it is** (see Proverbs 30:24-25).

8. **Be careful of borrowing.** Remember, the borrower is a slave to the lender (see Proverbs 22:7). Bad debts can destroy relationships and challenge your integrity.

While I have shared these lessons, I want to challenge you to go read books from experts about money management, eliminating debts, upgrading your money mindset, building wealth, investing, etc.

When you begin to steward God's resources God's way, you will be amazed at how God shows up in the most unexpected ways.

Story Time

I want to stress the importance of learning to better steward your money. But I can tell you that you don't need money to live and experience God's blessings and abundance.

God has been so faithful to me, not because I have always been a good person or because I made great money decisions, but simply because of His mercy and undeserving favor.

I struggled to decide which of the many testimonies to share of God showing up in supplying my needs, exceedingly blessing me, and supernatural provisions—from school fee provision miracles, getting a mortgage when I shouldn't be qualified, blessing me with trips paid for by others, having friends—even strangers—who blessed me with money and things unexpectedly, etc. I have many testimonies.

The final thing I want to leave with you in this chapter is to not be afraid to ask God for anything and everything. You might not get all your prayers answered, but still ask. Be honest with your motives, and when God blesses you, see how you can be a blessing to others. Never take the glory; instead, acknowledge God and be grateful for what you are currently blessed with.

Self-Check Prompts

What are some unhealthy habits you have regarding handling money?

_____

_____

_____

_____

_____

What is your biggest fear in relation to money?

_____

_____

_____

_____

_____

What do you want your financial life to look like ten years from now?

_____

_____

_____

_____

What is one thing you could do today to improve your financial life?

_____

_____

_____

_____

"You say, 'If I had a little more, I should be very satisfied.' You make a mistake. If you are not content with what you have, you would not be satisfied if it were doubled."
—Charles Haddon Spurgeon

Success Strategy #5

Get Better at Networking

"Many will seek the favor of a generous man, and every man is a friend to him who gives gifts." (Proverbs 19:6 – NASB).

Power Keys

- Networking is the process of developing and maintaining valuable relationships.
- Connections create opportunities.
- The time to be intentional about networking is NOW.
- Networking is crucial to your professional success.

If you truly desire to live a purposeful and impactful life, you cannot do it by yourself. It is crucial to connect with the right people.

As I reflect on my journey, I have seen how networking has expanded my influence and helped to position me for favorable opportunities. Let me put out this disclaimer: God doesn't need our help to give us favor, but He has called us to strive in community where each one reach one, so think of networking as you putting work to your faith.

Networking is powerful for career development, business success, ministry opportunities, and overall personal upliftment. So, this strategy can be a game-changer for you if you take faith steps to release any scarcity mindset holding you back from your abundance.

What networking is not:

- It is not asking someone for a job.
- It is not about bribing or smooching people.
- It is not about being an obsessive stalker.
- It is more than an event you attend to exchange business cards.

Networking is a process of developing and maintaining valuable relationships, which will enrich and empower you to achieve your goals.

- Networking takes time and is a process.
- Networking is a strategy for managing your career and boosting your business.
- It is a relationship that sees how you can help others; it is not a "me" focus.

Why should you network?

- To develop mutually beneficial relationships.
- It is still the #1 most effective way to land a job.
- You will gain information that will help you grow professionally.
- It will increase your knowledge of your industry so you can be a thought-leader.
- You will establish new business contacts to boost your visibility.

As I write this chapter, I remembered two particular experiences I wanted to share when I was a very young girl.

Growing up, I always heard I was a "chatterbox." All my reports would confirm that. Since I loved to talk, I wanted to be a lawyer. I was adamant that that was the path I would pursue. So, one day, when I was eleven years old, in 7th grade, walking downtown, I decided I was going to start learning more about my future career. Of course, I didn't know I was networking at the time.

I walked into a law office on Duke Street, introduced myself to the receptionist, and asked to speak to a lawyer because "one day I will become a lawyer, and I need to know from now what path I should take." I met a lawyer that day. She was dressed in black, looked so professional, and was so welcoming. She answered all my many questions. She was so impressed that this "young inner-city girl" had such big dreams, and she told me that I should keep connected with her, and she would do whatever she could to help me with my future career.

PS. I think I went back twice after that but didn't keep the connection because a few friends thought I was "too young to be so serious about my career." Silly me for listening.

Similarly, when I finished high school, I was encouraged to consider becoming an Actuary because I was very good at mathematics. One day, I looked in the phone directory and saw that there were only five actuarial companies in Jamaica at that time. I called each of them, explaining that I was a 6th former who desired to study actuarial science and wanted to know more from someone experienced in the field. Again, I was networking but didn't know I was.

A gentleman called back a few days later, saying he wanted to meet with me for lunch because he was so impressed that a young person would reach out to learn more about the career. It was a great lunch. He even offered me internship opportunities once I started college.

PS. At the end of the meeting, I felt like I couldn't bother with actuarial science and the many exams I needed to take after college. Silly me again. Well, maybe not!

So, how do you effectively network so you will gain and be a blessing to others?

DOs of networking:

- Take on volunteer positions.

- Visit and join associations and professional groups that will spark your interest or that you are passionate about.
- Follow through quickly on referrals.
- Be genuine and build trust and relationships.
- Become known as a resource to others.
- Ask open-ended questions in conversations.
- Have a clear understanding of what you do and what type of connections you need.
- Go beyond your industry.
- Listen to others.

Don'ts of networking:

- Do not bother your contacts constantly.
- Do not buy them expensive gifts to bribe them.
- Do not fear "big shots." People are people no matter what position they hold.
- Don't burden people with your personal life story.
- Don't judge people based on appearance or even titles.
- Don't drink too much at any business event.
- Don't build relationships with expectations. Be genuine.
- Don't take "NOs" personally.
- Don't be a pushy self-promoter.

Encouragement For Introverts

Many introverts shy away from networking because of fear, or they believe it doesn't fit their personality.

Being an introvert has advantages because they often spend more time listening and less time talking. This means they often notice details and remember facts. When they do engage, they are often more focused on others than themselves. Often, you will notice that someone who is an introvert changes when they start discussing topics they are passionate about.

Remember, networking is not a one-way street.

9 ways to become an effective networker:

1. Be yourself.
2. Do your research.
3. Find common ground.
4. Show respect for people's time.
5. Offer to help others.
6. Be a good listener.
7. Be available as a resource person.
8. Show appreciation.
9. Make others feel important through praising their good traits.

Networking Tips

- Ensure your email address is appropriate.
- Build a LinkedIn profile and update often.
- Create an appropriate Facebook page.
- Participate in discussion forums.
- Join organizations and business and professional networks, such as Rotary, Kiwanis, Lions Club, Toastmaster Community groups, Development groups, etc.
- Attend conferences, job fairs, and business events.
- Identify mentors and mentor someone.
- Volunteer your time and talents to worthy causes.
- Utilize alumni organizations.
- Set up information interviews.
- Utilize Facebook and LinkedIn groups.
- Watch and share articles, blogs, YouTube channels.

Networking can be a game-changer for your career and/or business.

Self-Check Prompts

What are the personal benefits you could gain if you become better at networking?

_____

_____

_____

What is your biggest struggle in networking with others?

What three steps can you take to upgrade your connections? Think about an organization you can get involved in or persons you can reach out to.

Why do you think networking can be so effective in increasing your impact?

"Networking is not about just connecting people. It's about connecting people with people, people with ideas, and people with opportunities."
—Michele Jennae

Success Strategy #6

Slay Your Goals

"The plans of the diligent lead surely to abundance and advantage, but everyone who acts in haste comes surely to poverty." (Proverbs 21:5 - AMP).

Power Keys

- God desires for you to fulfill His purpose; setting goals make the process more manageable.
- When you spend time delighting in God, you will begin to desire His desires.
- Faith turns your dreams into reality; goal-setting makes it easier.
- God's dream for your life is exponentially bigger than your dream.

A goal is a collection of actions that together lead to an outcome. A compelling goal is something that is meaningful to you.

63

From a biblical perspective, we approach goal-setting in a balanced way. Many don't set goals at all and live carefree with the excuse of "waiting" on God. Others set goals with no thoughts of God and are laser-focused on worldly accomplishment only. Both approaches are extremes that will lead to a dissatisfied and purposeless life.

Effective Goal-Setting Tips

1. **You need to be flexible:** You must be willing to change your plans when they need to be changed (see Proverbs 13:17).

2. **Plan for tomorrow but live in today:** You must have a fine balance in your life between planning for the future and living for today (see Matthew 6:34).

3. **Don't try to set too many goals:** You need to be focused on completing one major goal at a time (see Proverbs 4:25).

4. **Recognize that God is greater than your plans:** God has the right at any time to change your plans around. Your plan may not be His plan. God has a better idea (see Proverbs 16:1).

5. Set goals that give a holistic perspective of who you want to become and what you want to achieve.

"Where there is no revelation, people cast off restraint; but blessed is the one who heeds wisdom's instruction." (Proverbs 29:18 - NIV).

Become a Finisher

Are you someone who starts a lot of projects but rarely finishes them?

I felt it was important to add this encouragement to you that goal-setting is pointless if you keep starting things and never complete them. Part of success is being committed to finishing what you start.

People often struggle with becoming a finisher because they have multiple passions and are not sure how to keep focused. They are also easily distracted, are chronic multitaskers, and allow fear of success or failure to cripple them.

Here are some tips to finish your goals strong:

- Develop a routine and cultivate healthy success habits.
- Sharpen your focus to decrease distractions.
- Make a commitment to finish what you start.
- Have accountability and surround yourself with other goal-getters.
- Learn to practice completing smaller tasks.
- Constantly visualize what success would look like.

65

- Be real with yourself about challenges and expect obstacles. Develop a persevering spirit to keep you motivated.
- Keep feeding yourself positive, affirming, and motivating messages.

Goal-setting is a habit you have to develop. For some people, it comes more naturally, especially if you have the gift of administration. For others, it is something you become intentional with learning and consistently practice to become better, like riding a bicycle.

Story Time

I have always been a natural go-getter. As young as nine, I remember writing in my diary about which high school I wanted to attend, what rank I aimed to achieve in my class, and even outlining my career goals.

When I became more intentional about cultivating a relationship with God and pursuing my purpose, goal-setting became even more important, especially as the seasons changed. My goals are holistic (personal, spiritual, financial, professional, health, etc.) This helps me to maintain balance.

People ask me daily how I accomplish so much. One thing I try not to do is complain about a lack of time but to steward my time as best as possible. So every year I set annual goals, then I set quarterly goals, then I have monthly goals, then I write my weekly goals and daily journal my to-achieve tasks. This may seem extreme but believe me, it is liberating and helps to remain focused.

Just like any habit, it takes practice and intentionality to be consistent if you want to slay your goals so you can become more purposeful and impactful and live abundantly. You must be willing to do something different if what you are currently doing is not working.

I also keep a record of small and big goals achieved, and I celebrate everything. If I get a podcast interview, it is something to celebrate. If I am consistent with exercising for a week, I celebrate. I realize that this life is a gift, and tomorrow is not promised to me. Life can change in the blink of an eye, and I keep these thoughts at the forefront of my thoughts.

My final encouragement to you: if you make mistakes in setting goals, it is okay. God desires for you to be in His will, so He will lead you in the way you should go as you walk in faith (see Psalm 32:8).

Self-Check Prompts

What is one huge goal you have for yourself in the next twelve months?

_____

_____

_____

_____

_____

How will your dreams contribute to impacting the kingdom?

_____

_____

_____

_____

What resources do you need to achieve your goals to live the experiences you desire?

_____

_____

_____

_____

Spend some quiet time with God, seeking Him about your dreams. Ask Him for direction, clarity, and wisdom.

_____

_____

_____

_____

_____

".... because goals are the map that will guide you toward your God-given purpose, without setting them, you will also wander in circles without getting where you need to go."
—Shana Schutte

Success Strategy #7

Dress For The Dream

"... she dresses in fine linen and purple gowns." (Proverbs 31:22b – NLT).

Power Keys

- People do judge a book by its cover.
- Dress not for where you are but where you desire to be.
- You don't have to be rich to be chic.
- As royalty, you should look like it.

I am shocked to be writing a chapter about dressing because I don't think I am the most fashionable person. I mean, I like to look nice and enjoy being complimented on how beautiful I look, but I don't think I have much fashion tips to share.

As I prayed to outline this book, I felt it was very important to include this as a success strategy. We always hear that we shouldn't judge a book by its cover, but the reality is, we do. Even the Bible tells us that God looks at the heart, but men (women) look at the outward appearance (see 1 Samuel 16:7). So, how we dress affects us.

I grew up being a bit tomboyish, yet I loved to dress skimpy. Doesn't make sense, right? I remember working at the bank (my first job), and I struggled with the dress code. For one, I was poor, so my mom had to make a few outfits for me. They were okay but not as nice as the other ladies in the bank. Next, I struggled to be on 'fleek' every day. I was that type of girl who gets up and hit the road without even brushing my hair—don't judge me. Yes, I was ambitious, but the idea of dressing up every day was too much work, and I used to think it didn't take all of that. I eventually realized that most of these practices were based on my scarcity mindset.

Thank God, as I got older and grew professionally, I improved. I was also a pageant girl, so I learned some tips about grooming. I love my six-inch stilettos, so I managed to look pretty decent.

Then, when I became an entrepreneur, I realized I had to level up. One of the things God told me to do before I released my first book was to do a professional photoshoot. He directed me to the makeup artiste, how my hair should be done, and the photographer I should use. It was quite pricey, but it was one of my best investments.

When I started to dress, not for where I was (because I was broke) but for where I wanted to go (abundance), my platform, brand, and influence drastically grew.

Here are five simple yet cost-effective ways to level up your style:

1. **Learn to apply basic makeup:** Didn't I confess that I'm still learning? While paying makeup artists for professional outings and shoots is great, you won't always have the money to pay someone to ensure your makeup is on fleek. Also, you might end up in situations where you can't get anyone, so learning basic makeup is a very good investment in your brand.

2. **Go thrift shopping:** This simply means there are stores where you can find really nice outfits—even designer ones—for reasonable prices.

3. **Learn to walk in high heels and invest in a nice pair:** Listen, there are certain places you will go where you need those stilettos to help you stand out. Mind you, I am a big shoe-lover so I tend to have tons of heels, but I can tell you, even the simplest outfits get leveled up in those pumps. Oh yes, practice to walk in them, okay; wobbling and tripping ain't cute.

4. **Unless you have money, stay away from buying too many trendy items:** Trends change so often, so stick to outfits that are simpler yet chic.

   PS. I still wear my high school graduation dress and get compliments even after over twenty years. Don't ask why I have a 20-year-old dress in my closet; it is just a timeless piece.

5. **Ask for help:** Yes, that is a tip. As I said, I am not the most fashionista person when it comes to style, so I have Opal, my fashionista mom, Nadine, and some friends who are. If you are struggling with what to wear, ask someone you admire or you know is more stylish.

Another tip that is unpopular, maybe even weird, but I do very often is to ask the Holy Spirit. Like, seriously, I do ask God what to wear, how to do my hair, etc., and He answers because He cares about even the supposedly "small" things that are important to me.

Again, these are things I am still trying to be consistent with.

This chapter is really an encouragement and not to give fashion tips or a guide on how to dress. Sorry, that is not my gift at all. I just want you to know that how you dress and how you carry yourself is a part of the abundance lifestyle you desire. You can't declare yourself to be royalty and look like a peasant; the devil is a liar. Your confidence level

74

increases, and your insecurity decreases when you know you are out and looking like the queen you truly are.

Self-Check Prompts

Name three people you admire their style and what you like about it.

_____

_____

_____

_____

_____

What in your closet do you need to get rid of? Start now!

_____

_____

_____

_____

When do you feel the most successful? Are you in the right place, doing exactly what you are supposed to be doing?

_____

_____

_____

What can you learn to do that will help you upgrade your style permanently?

"The secret to style is a beautiful smile."
—Richelle E. Goodrich

Success Strategy #8

Take Fast Action

"But someone will say, "One person has faith, another has actions." My answer is, "Show me how anyone can have faith without actions. I will show you my faith by my actions." (James 2:18 – GNT).

Power Keys

- Clarity comes through action.
- Action creates habits that lead to success.
- Overthinking delays your progress.
- Taking fast action will stretch your faith.

The truth is, many people don't lack information. Many people desire to change the world, and many actually know what to do. The sad part is, many don't experience the blessings and abundance that is possible for them because they never take action on their ideas.

77

Have you ever had an idea that you wrote down and you probably even shared it with a friend? Then, months pass, and you keep waiting for the perfect time, but then you see someone launch your idea. Well, I have experienced that. Believe me, it is heartbreaking.

In 2016, I felt a deep desire to start a business. I took action to hire my first business coach. I was in the process of publishing my first book and in discovering my passions, she suggested I help people publish their books. That sounded crazy to me since I was paying someone to publish my book. Plus, I had done quite a few self-publishing courses, and I realized that I just didn't have the interest in doing all that by myself.

Eventually, I prayed about it and started researching. I felt like God was leading me in the right direction. I took action to prepare packages, hired a lawyer to prepare contracts, and put resources together. The Lord even gave me the name, DayeLight Publishers, a slogan "It's Saving Time" and told me not to take royalties. I had never heard that before, so I knew it was God. I put all the information together, then sat on it for months. One day, I went on social media to a horrific surprise: someone I looked up to had launched their publishing company with the same exact idea. To say I was depressed would be an understatement.

Since that experience, I have tried my very best to take action on my ideas quickly. I don't wait for it to be perfect; I was willing to learn along the way.

No matter how amazing your idea is; no matter how great your goal is; no matter how impactful your vision can be, if you don't take action, nothing will happen.

One of the hindrances to our taking action is that we fear change. Most times, we become so comfortable where we are. Even though we desire more, we fear feeling uncomfortable.

Here are three tips for taking action:

1. **Start where you are:** You are equipped with enough to get started. As you take small action, you can grow as you go. While there will probably be a need for development, once you get started, your confidence will grow.

2. **Don't try to do too much at once:** Don't be overwhelmed with trying to get too many things done. Make a list of steps you should take towards that goal, then pace yourself as you take small steps.

3. **Take the first step now:** This is usually the hardest part of the journey. Think about all the positive outcomes that can happen when you step out in faith and focus on this to keep you encouraged.

One thing about taking fast action is that you have less time to think about all the things that could go wrong. There is a BLESSING attached to fast action.

Run with your ideas. Action will always take you closer to your goals. Inaction is a dream killer. Step out in FAITH. Remember, your faith pleases God.

Self-Check Prompts

What is your greatest fear when it comes to taking action toward your goals?

_____

_____

_____

_____

_____

What is one new habit you need to adapt that will help you create a successful lifestyle?

_____

_____

_____

_____

_____

_____

Name one action step you can take in the next 24 hours towards your dreams.

_____

_____

_____

_____

_____

Imagine you had an ideal month; what three things did you complete?

_____

_____

_____

_____

_____

"At the end of the day, you are the only one that is limiting your ability to dream, or to actually execute on your dreams. Don't let yourself get in the way of that."
—Falon Fatemi

Success Strategy #9

Invest in Your Growth

"Intelligent people are always ready to learn. Their ears are open for knowledge." (Proverbs 18:15 - NLT).

Power Keys

- Investing in your personal growth increases your confidence and focus.
- The best investment you can make is in yourself. It will improve your life and those around you.
- To fulfill your potential, accomplish big goals, and make an impact, start by investing in your growth.
- When you develop a passion for learning, you will never cease to grow.

Your personal development is a major key to success. You must become a life-long learner so you can grow and become a better version of

83

yourself. When I talk about personal development, this includes your spiritual, professional, and self-growth.

Your self-development includes your personal skills, competencies, and knowledge. The idea that you will finish high school or college and that is all the learning you need is you placing a cap on your capabilities. Learning is not just about getting more qualifications, even though this is great for personal fulfillment and career advancement; there are other ways to grow.

Self-development enhances your personal effectiveness, and that can help in areas such as cultivating better habits, managing stress, improving communication, developing a better self-image, increasing self-awareness, etc. Being intentional with growing in these areas will result in improving your quality of life.

The more you invest in your growth (spiritually, personally, and professionally), the more your confidence increases, which helps you attract blessings beyond your limitations. You will also realize how motivated you become to go after your goals and dreams, and you will be more resilient to overcome struggles and obstacles in life.

When you invest in your personal growth, you develop characteristics that result in living a blessed, purposeful, and abundant life.

Ways To Invest In Your Spiritual Growth

1. Become a student of the Word of God. Read the Bible, obey God's commands, and receive His promises.
2. Spend time in personal devotions and quiet time with God.
3. Fellowship with other believers.
4. Be willing to be disciplined and mentored.
5. Listen and read faith-building messages. Attend church, watch YouTube videos, read blogs, read books from Christian authors, listen to podcasts, etc.
6. Serve and utilize your spiritual gifts by evangelizing, going on ministry trips, joining ministries at your church, volunteering in your community, etc.

Ways To Invest In Your Professional Growth

1. Read books in your industry.
2. Hire a coach or mentor.
3. Earn additional certifications.
4. Build your brand.
5. Do career-planning sessions.
6. Network with other professionals.

Ways To Invest In Your Self-Development

1. Pray and journal often.
2. Practice gratitude.

3. Read personal development books.
4. Watch less TV and listen to more motivational messages.
5. Spend time with your loved ones.
6. Choose your friends wisely.
7. Find a mentor or hire a life coach.
8. Eat healthy and practice self-care.
9. Exercise and do physical activities.
10. Learn a new skill or take a class to learn a new hobby.
11. Learn a new language.
12. Practice setting goals.
13. Get rest and sleep well.
14. Drink lots of water.
15. Learn to steward your finances.
16. Practice forgiveness.
17. Dream big and visualize your future.
18. Don't compare yourself, and don't try to please others.
19. Dress well and practice proper hygiene.
20. Travel and gain new experiences.

"Let the wise hear and increase in learning, and the one who understands obtain guidance." (Proverbs 1:5 – ESV).

Self-Check Prompts

Name three ways you can start investing in your growth (spiritually, personally, or professionally)?

When do you feel most confident in yourself, and when do you feel the least confident?

What is your biggest insecurity? How can you overcome it?

What do you really want in life? What are three steps you can take today to start making that happen?

_____

_____

_____

"Income seldom exceeds personal development."
—Jim Rohn

Success Strategy #10

Share Your Story

"They overcame him because of the Lamb's blood, and because of the word of their testimony." (Revelations 12:11a – KJV).

Power Keys

- Sharing your story will inspire hope in others who may be going through something similar.
- God wants you to share your story and testify of His goodness.
- Through sharing stories, we connect with each other.
- The world needs your message because it is unique and can bless others.

Story Time

After I recommitted my life to the Lord in 2014, I felt this burden to share my testimony on social media. Of course, it was a struggle initially because I was concerned about what others would say or think about me.

Through reading other blogs, I felt inspired to be authentic about my mistakes, struggles, successes, and life lessons with the aim of empowering others.

Fast forward to today: I am a multi-bestselling author, award-winning talk show host, top-rated publisher, international speaker, and the best coach ever who has helped thousands of people share their stories and have built my empowerment empire around my passion for writing, speaking, and coaching.

I truly believe we all have a message to share with the world. Your message includes your testimony, lessons, and the good news of salvation.

While there are people who have shared many powerful stories of overcoming struggles and have impacted lives globally, for me, without Christ getting the glory, it won't have eternal impact. As a believer, that is the most important purpose of life: giving God glory in your story.

My journey started with sharing testimonies on social media; then the Lord led me to start a blog. My blog is titled

"Chosen Vessel." Go read how far God has taken me from @ http://chosenvessel15.blogspot.com. From that blog, I wrote my first book, *Living A Royal Reality: Discovering Your Identity, Purpose and Worth in Christ.* My platform has definitely grown tremendously since then. Now I am the host of The Ambitious Jesus Girl Podcast (formerly the Diary Of A Jesus Girl Podcast) and The DayeLight Show (my own talk show aired on MTM TV). These platforms allow me to continue sharing my message and the story of other kingdom persons all over the world.

That is my journey, but here is the thing: God desires you to share your story also.

A BLESSED life comes from living a life that is not about you. Allowing God to use you for His glory and sharing your story is a part of that. God never wastes pain; He says He will give you beauty for ashes and work all things together for your good (see Isaiah 61:3 and Romans 8:28). So, no matter what your past was, in Christ, you are a new creation.

3 Reasons You Should Share Your Story

1. It helps you heal and find freedom where you can see how your lessons can indeed be a blessing to someone else.

91

2. It will help you find meaning, even in the most painful moments of your life. You will gain a greater sense of purpose, clarity, and direction.

3. It will help you find your voice. You will learn how to communicate in a way that is authentically you.

"Sharing our truths can provide the opportunity for great healing."
—Kristen Noel

How to Find the Courage to Share Your Story

1. Be true to who you are. Remember that your authenticity is your superpower.

2. Remember, shame cannot kill you, and guilt has no power over you—Jesus set you free.

3. There is nothing new under the sun, so nothing you have been through is unique only to you. What is unique is how you share it to bless others.

4. Remember, it is not about you but how God desires to use you to impact others.

5. Do the work to get the healing you need. Go to counseling, hire a coach, journal, cry, forgive others, forgive yourself, let go of bitterness, and believe God can use you.

6. Don't be defined by your mistakes. Know that your identity is found in Jesus Christ, and you are the apple of His eye.

7. Focus on the lessons you learnt, and share transparently how you have grown in that area.

The courage it takes to share your story might be the very thing someone else needs to open their heart to hope.

Healing from your past is very important before you share your story. Deal with any unforgiveness or bitterness that may allow you to fall apart when you are sharing.

Ways To Share Your Story

1. Publish a book
2. Email newsletter
3. WhatsApp motivational messages
4. Podcast
5. Blogging
6. Live video or vlogging
7. Mentor others
8. Become a life coach
9. Motivational speaking
10. Contribute to magazines
11. Social media platforms
12. Launch an inspirational product line
13. YouTube
14. Write poems

15. Record a song

You may think this doesn't apply to you because you have not had any traumatic, dramatic, or difficult experiences. As a result, you convince yourself you have nothing to share with others. But that is not true.

Life offers us values and experiences that are rich with the potential to teach lessons. To bless others, we must be willing to share these insights, shifting the focus away from ourselves and toward the impact we can have on those around us.

Self-Check Prompts

Why do you want to share your story? Or why do you think you should share your message?

_____

_____

_____

_____

_____

Who will benefit from your story?

_____

_____

_____

_____

_____

What is one significant lesson you have learnt in life after a tragedy?

_____

_____

_____

_____

_____

What have you achieved success in that can inspire others?

_____

_____

_____

_____

_____

"The two most important days in your life are the day you are born and the day you find out why."
—Mark Twain

Success Strategy #11

Practice Self-Care

> "Six days you shall labor, but on the seventh day you shall rest; even during the plowing season and harvest you must rest." (Exodus 34:21 – ESV).

Power Keys

- Busyness doesn't mean productivity. Productivity leads to impact. Busyness leads to burnout.
- Learn how to say "no" to things that over-extend you and start making time for things that matter more.
- Practicing self-care and wellness is no longer a luxury; it is a must.
- Incorporate self-care activities daily.

Self-care has become a trendy topic online these days, and that is not bad because it means many are seeing the importance of cultivating healthy practices. This includes being intentional about taking care of yourself

97

physically, emotionally, and spiritually, which impacts how you truly live abundantly and how you are able to impact others.

Personally, I see self-care as simply being a good steward of the body God has blessed me with. Many ambitious and purpose-driven women tend to push themselves to achieve certain goals. In going hard to accomplish our dreams, we tend to forget we have limitations; God has designed us in such a way that when we reach our limit, it truly affects us, which is known as "burnout."

In a culture that glorifies busyness, grinding, and flaunting, we often get into the rat race of constantly chasing after material possessions and worldly accolades.

Here are four areas you should think about when cultivating a habit of proper self-care:

- **Your spirit:** Are you ensuring that your soul is prospering? For example, ensure your heart is free of hatred, anger, grudges, and other forms of negative emotions. All of these hinder your healing and blessings.

- **Your mindset:** Are you allowing negative thoughts to bombard your mind? For example, be mindful of your self-talk. For example, replace *"I will never be able to do this"* with *"I will learn from this* *experience."* Also, practice gratitude by focusing on the good things, no matter how small they seem.

- **Your emotions:** Are you journaling your feelings and experiences to allow you to be in the moment and capture emotional moments? For example, process your emotions by identifying, accepting, and releasing them. This gives you greater awareness.

- **Your body:** How have you been fueling your body to help you be your best in this season? For example, stay hydrated by drinking water, moving your body by engaging in physical activities like walking, exercising, swimming, etc., and trying to eat properly.

Examples of Self-Care and Wellness Activities

- Pay attention to your physical health
- Get enough sleep
- Eat healthier
- Drink lots of water
- Take vitamins and supplement
- Rest
- Get a massage with essential oils
- Keep a daily journal and be totally honest about your feelings
- Let yourself cry when you need to
- Deliberately encourage yourself to laugh with old memories or funny videos

- Take nature walks
- Practice daily gratitude
- Listen to worship music
- Make a list of 5-10 things that make you feel alive, then ask yourself how you can better incorporate these things into your life
- Say affirmations
- Go to the movie alone
- Volunteer for a charity
- Journal often
- See a therapist
- Hire a life coach
- Read more books and inspiring quotes
- Make a self-care box filled with materials such as candles, essential oils, affirmation cards, self-care ideas, a book, etc.
- Smile at yourself in the mirror

"Practicing self-care and wellness is no longer a luxury; it's a must. Self-care is crucial to your success because your body needs a break, your creativity needs a boost and your mindset needs to bloom."
—Stacia Pierce

Self-Check Prompts

What is one self-care activity you are going to do for yourself every day?

_____

_____

_____

_____

_____

If you struggle with self-care, what are the top reasons you neglect taking care of yourself?

_____

_____

_____

_____

_____

How are you ensuring your soul prospers?

_____

_____

_____

_____

_____

Success Strategy #12

Build BRAND U

"For we are God's handiwork, created in Christ Jesus to do good works, which God prepared in advance for us to do." (Ephesians 2:10 – NIV).

Power Keys

- A purposeful brand doesn't just happen; it must be intentional.
- Authenticity is the secret to building an impactful brand.
- You are a brand, whether you like it or not.
- Your story makes you unique and differentiates you from others doing similar things.

Confession

Personal branding is one of my favorite topics to talk about. When I started to learn the value of honing a personal brand, how I approach life, business, and even my ministry shifted.

This success strategy is important because when you become intentional about honing your personal brand, you will see an increase in blessings, bookings, and boundless opportunities.

A brand is how a person feels about you and your company. It is not what you think about you and your business but what others think. There has been a drastic increase in the awareness and importance of building a personal brand for persons who desire to make an impact, such as entrepreneurs, leaders, professionals, and even ministers.

Branding is the secret ingredient that boosts visibility, credibility, and loyalty among the audience you desire to serve.

Branding is more than a logo, website, and colors; it is how you are perceived. While you can't control people's opinion of you, you can influence with what you put out there consistently. So, whether you like it or not—know it or not—you are a BRAND. The sooner you accept this, the greater your chance to build a successful business, ministry, or career.

Story Time

In January 2016, I was having a meeting with a few of my dear friends and accountability partners regarding a ministry I founded. After rededicating my life to Jesus Christ in January 2014, I had grown in zeal and passion for sharing the gospel. So, I would share inspirational words—mostly edge-snatching and convicting—daily as I learned more about what surrendering to Christ and living a life of faith really meant.

In this meeting, my "unfiltered" friend, Dez, said to me, *"Crystal, you're a brand, and you need to start being more conscious of that."* At that moment, I got so mad. How could one of my closest friends say something so insulting to me? Every time I think about my ignorance, I cringe.

The truth is, when she referred to me as a BRAND, I thought she was saying, *"I was doing ministry for my own personal motives,"* or *"I was trying to make money for the gospel,"* or *"I was seeking a stage to build my own platform and not promote Christ."* I thought she was telling me I was being worldly. For us Jesus girls—a.k.a. women after God's heart—the last thing someone should accuse us of is being worldly when God calls us to be separated from the world (see 1 John 2:15). Here's why I also thought this: these were things I was accused of, either by the enemy, my personal insecurities or, yes, other Christian women.

Fast forward to eight years later: I am now a proud Brand Strategist—one of my many titles and calling—who loves Jesus, aims to build a profitable global business, and I am still passionate about ministering the gospel.

Over the last few years, God had to renew my religious mindset as I thought building a platform, honing my personal brand, charging for my services, and growing my influence were ungodly and un-Christlike. I have learnt how to properly steward my gifts and calling so I can build the kingdom and give God glory.

6 Essentials for Honing Your Personal Brand

Honing your personal brand is about seeking clarity on your calling and purpose. This influences your career, business, and even your life. Once you have this clarity, you can set out on your faith journey to impact others in confidence because you know where you are going and how to get there.

B – Build your brand through social media.
R – Recognize your expertise.
A – Authenticity is your superpower.
N – Network and connect with others.
D – Design a stylish and smart identity (your visual brand is also important).
U – Unique (what makes you special? What makes you stand out?).

Branding Tips for Career Professionals

- Develop your expertise.
- Be consistent with your appearance.
- Update your LinkedIn profile.
- Ensure your social media is consistent with what you want your employers to know about you.

Branding Tips for Entrepreneurs

- Know your target audience and niche.
- Purchase your personal domain name.
- Provide excellent customer service.
- Share your story to connect with your audience.

Branding Tips for Ministers

- Take professional photos and operate in excellence.
- Collaborate with other ministers. There is no competition in the kingdom.
- Utilize digital platforms to spread the gospel.
- Build a community with the audience God has called you to serve.

Here are a few of my favorite personal branding quotes:

"Your personal brand is simply the public expression of your calling."

—*Mike Loomis*

"Building a brand means knowing your story and building and sharing that story."
—*T. McCleary*

"Your personal brand is what people say about you when you are not in the room."
—*C. Ducker*

"A brand is the set of expectations, memories, stories and relationships that, taken together, account for a consumer's decision to choose one product or service over another."
—*Seth Godin*

"The keys to brand success are self-definition, transparency, authenticity and accountability."
—*S. Mainwaring*

"Start by knowing what you want and who you are, build credibility around it and deliver it online in a compelling way."
—*Krista Neher*

Crafting Your Personal Purpose Statement

A personal purpose statement is a brief description of what you want to focus on, what you want to accomplish, and who you want to become.

Step 1 – Choose two actions—What you feel most called to do:

_____

_____

_____

Step 2 – Determine your core values—What principles you stand for:

_____

_____

_____

Step 3 – Select a recipient—Who you feel called to serve:

_____

_____

_____

Step 4 – Put the pieces together, for example, My purpose is to:

_____

_____

_____

_____

A good example is: ***To create opportunities for today's youth.***

Self-Check Prompts

What makes you unique?

What are your strengths?

Which skills or capabilities are you most proud of?

What are you working toward/have accomplished that gives you a sense of purpose?

Success Strategy #13

Become An Expert

"The heart of the discerning acquires knowledge, for the ears of the wise seek it out." (Proverbs 18:15 – NIV).

Power Keys

- Being seen as an expert increases your opportunities.
- Your brand amplifies with expert status.
- **F.O.C.U.S: F**ollow **O**ne **C**ourse **U**ntil **S**uccessful.
- You will position yourself for wealth when you are an expert.

This book is about helping you to have an impact and about you accessing abundance, right? Well, in today's economy, you must *become an expert*. We are in an information era, where we have access to people all over the world because of the internet. Of course, this is amazing because we are now able to expand our influence over borders. But it also forces us to find ways to

113

differentiate ourselves. One such way is to become an expert.

Being an expert is not just about getting qualifications but increasing our knowledge in a particular area (or two) to boost our confidence in an area we want to contribute to. This is important if you are trying to build a successful career or business.

7 Reasons You Should Become an Expert

1. It increases your confidence level.
2. You don't have to chase opportunities; you will attract opportunities.
3. You will earn more money. Think about what you pay a general doctor practitioner versus what you pay to visit the gynaecologist.
4. People question your capabilities less.
5. It will boost your visibility and make you stand out.
6. You increase your network.
7. You will be seen as a thought-leader who can be trusted.

As a woman who used to pride herself in being a jill-of-all trades, I can say my hesitance to really become an expert in fewer areas has impacted my business tremendously, especially as I build an online platform. So, I am trying to help you make the decision not to be a generalist but to become a specialist.

Here are three things I want you to note about being an expert:

i. **You don't have to know everything about a subject to be an expert.** You just need to know enough that you can share with someone else. Think about someone who is in Grade 9. They can teach persons in Grade 1-8. So, if you are at Level 5, focus on helping Levels 4 and under. Don't worry about Level 6 and over. Walk in your lane and own it.

ii. **There will always be someone who knows more than you.** Don't be threatened but be inspired that you can get there too. For now, do you, boo.

iii. **There are people who know far less or don't even know anything about that topic and want to learn.** Again, your gift is needed in this world. Stop holding back!

PS. You can become an expert through knowledge, experience, curiosity, or an innate gift from God.

So, how can you become an expert:

1. **Focus on one subject/topic/area/industry at a time.** I don't know what you want to be considered an expert for but choose something you are passionate about and F.O.C.U.S: Follow One Course Until Successful.

2. **Become a perpetual learner.** Invest in books, courses, conferences, etc. We talked about that in Strategy #9.

3. **Start teaching or mentoring others.** Start sharing your knowledge on various platforms or with others. You will be impressed by how much you can impact someone by practicing.

4. **Just do it!** Stop overthinking.

Like branding, I don't believe because a term or concept is not specifically found in the Bible, it means it is not helpful or ungodly. Whether we choose to accept it or not, the Bible teaches that each of us has been given unique gifts, and no one possesses all the gifts *(see Romans 12:3-8 and 1 Corinthians 12:1-11)*. Some people will be better and more drawn to some topics that we just don't have a clue about, so we need their help.

Choose to develop your skillset and increase your knowledge to be seen as an expert. This is you being a good steward of the "talents" God has blessed you with. Remember, God is expecting returns on His investment in you (see Matthew 25:14-30).

If you are a believer, stop looking at certain things as being more spiritual than others. Often, we make it seem like if someone talks as an expert on godly marriage, they are more "spiritual" than someone who teaches about makeup. Nah!

116

We need each other, so again I say, do you, boo. Do whatever Jesus tells you to do.

Self-Check Prompts

What do you want to be known for? Consider what you want people to turn to you for guidance or answers.

What are three areas you feel passionate talking and learning about?

How can you start today to grow your expertise?

_____

_____

What skills/knowledge/gifts has God blessed you with that you feel you have buried instead of invested in?

_____

_____

_____

_____

_____

"The capacity to learn is a gift; the ability to learn is a skill; the willingness to learn is a choice."
—Brian Herbert

Success Strategy #14

Monetize Your Skills

"People curse the one who hoards grain, but they pray God's blessing on the one who is willing to sell." (Proverbs 11:26 – NIV).

Power Keys

- It is okay to desire to make money; nothing is ungodly about it.
- Your skills can be used to start a business or side hustle.
- You start a business to provide a solution.
- Multiple streams of income are no longer a luxury; they have become a necessity.

This book is written to share on abundance, right? Honestly, can we live a truly abundant life without financial blessings?

In Strategy #4, I shared about stewarding your finances. Often, we hear about stewardship with a focus on "cutting back." Let me remind you that increasing your income is an essential aspect of stewardship. Here's the truth: we have the potential to create multiple streams of income. We possess amazing business ideas and the power to generate greater wealth for ourselves and our families. What we lack is the *"know-how."* As Hosea 4:6 says, the people perish because of a lack of knowledge.

In this chapter, I want to share some tools and tips with you to make money from your skills and use your gifts to start a striving business.

Story Time

I was introduced to the concept of entrepreneurship in grade 9 while studying the subject Principles of Business. I continued my studies up to the master's level in business because I was very good at it, and I eventually realized it was a part of my God-given calling.

Even though I always wanted to start my own business, I honestly did not have the confidence that I really could. I also didn't consider myself a big risk-taker, so I decided to settle on building a career.

I look back on the many days my siblings and I would spend hours talking and planning which business venture we would launch. I was always a visionary who saw money-making opportunities but would never consider actually launching them. So, again, I focused on building a corporate career and buried my entrepreneurial desires deep within.

While doing my master's in business administration, I had to do Essentials to Entrepreneurship. On the first day of the class, the lecturer asked who wanted to start their own business, and I was the only person in the class who didn't raise my hand. She challenged me by saying that by the end of the course, I would change my mind because of the incredible possibilities available to entrepreneurs. By the end of the term, when she asked again, my answer remained the same. I knew it was really a lie, but I was too afraid to consider the possibility.

Fast forward eight years later, I now operate three businesses, and I am sure there are more to come. What changed? God. No, seriously, when I surrendered my life to Jesus Christ and sought Him about my purpose, I got the revelation that this was a part of His plan for my life, and that gave me the courage to obey and believe it was possible.

While entrepreneurship has been really challenging, it really has been extremely fulfilling. It is a part of my Blessed, Booked, and Boundless journey.

Here is what I want you to know: if you truly desire to monetize your gifts, it is possible. Abundance means accessing everything God has in store for you, and financial blessings is a part of that, no matter what churchy folks may say.

Let's dive in.

6 Steps to Monetizing Your Skills

1. Identify your skillsets.
2. Identify and define your ideal customers (Who you can serve).
3. Identify the problem your skills will solve.
4. Create a product/service to fill your customers' needs.
5. Outline ways you will market your product/service.
6. Ensure your business/side hustle is aligned with your values or purpose.

Market Research is Crucial

To successfully launch anything as an entrepreneur, you must spend time doing research so you can know what people really need. In your research, focus on industry trends and spending behaviors, and carefully consider how you can offer something unique.

The truth is, there really is nothing new under the sun, so most likely, whatever you come up with, a version like it already exists. However, you can always find a way to improve it and offer your ideal customers value that they are willing to pay for.

Think about companies like Uber; it is not that taxi services didn't always exist, but they revolutionized the industry by adding something unique that made people's lives easier.

Sometimes you will have ideas you think are the best, but when you put it out there, people just aren't interested in spending money on that, or sometimes you are offering it to the wrong people. Again, this is why some type of marketing research is key to your success when monetizing your skills.

Entrepreneurial Tips

1. **Upgrade your money mindset.** This starts by asking yourself, *"Do I even believe I can make money from my skills (knowledge, experience, message, gifts)?"* If you don't believe, then it won't happen. So, start by dealing with your limiting beliefs around money, and spend time researching your ideas. Remember, your money-mindset is key to increasing your wealth.

2. **Don't try to figure it out by yourself; hire help to accomplish your goals quicker.** Starting a business is not for the faint-hearted, but I believe everyone who desires to can have a side business to increase their disposable income and generate long-term

wealth. The idea that we need to be "self-made" is foolish because there are people who know more about certain areas that will help accelerate our success. Don't allow pride to have you trying to figure out everything alone. Hire help!

3. **Be comfortable with standing out.** Here's the thing: as a solopreneur (i.e. if you are the only person operating your business now), it is a possibility that you have to put yourself out there. Putting yourself out there causes its own struggles for so many people because they worry about what others will say. Maybe you have been told you talk too much or you are too extra, so you automatically feel like shrinking back because you are tired of hearing those "insults." Maybe you have considered yourself "introverted, shy, humble," whatever the word you use to describe yourself, so you hold back from doing what you love, yet deep down, you desire to do something you are great at. I know it seems easier to hide, but here is Jesus' question to you: *"Who lights a lamp and put it under a bushel?" (see Matthew 5:13-16).* You have something to offer the world, so you need to forget about people and just do it.

4. **Ask for the sale.** As entrepreneurs, we often promote our products, but we don't give customers a clear call to action. People act quicker when they get clear instructions, so ensure you are asking for the sale.

5. **Keep your day job.** I know it is weird coming from a full-time entrepreneur, but the truth is, you need money to help fund your business idea. Avoid the pressure of being stressed over how your bills will be paid while you are building your business. Also, your job is your biggest investor. You can use the money you earn for things like marketing or branding, etc.

Honestly, I love to talk about business and teach about business because I have personal experience of the blessings, how impactful it is to serve others with my gifts, and how their lives have been tremendously blessed because of my product/service.

I know money is a very uncomfortable conversation to have with religious people, but I can tell you that having money to do all the projects I desired to do has been impactful. So, if you desire to monetize your gift, do so unapologetically, and believe me, you will be so happy you did.

Self-Check Prompts

List five skills you have that you are good at that people commend you for:

_____

_____

_____

125

_____

_____

What is your biggest fear when it comes to starting a business? If you already have a business, who do you need to hire to help you grow your revenue?

_____

_____

_____

_____

_____

Make a list of twenty ways you can make money in the next ninety days:

_____

_____

_____

_____

_____

What excuse have you been making to start your business? How are you holding yourself back from your financial blessing?

_____

_____

_____

_____

_____

Be an amateur. Not everything you do has to be good, especially at first."
—Ann Handley

Success Strategy #15

Don't Fear Failure

"The godly may trip seven times, but they will get up again. But one disaster is enough to overthrow the wicked." (Proverbs 24:16 – NIV).

Power Keys

- You failing doesn't make you a failure.
- Failing is an activity; don't accept it as a part of your identity.
- Failure is only permanent if you stay down and do not try again.
- God's opinion of you is what matters most. Remind yourself daily of His words and promises about you.

Have you ever been so afraid of failing at something that you don't even try at all?

The fear of failing is a reality for many people. There is a part of us that know we are destined for more, but we get crippled when we imagine that things might not go the most favorable way, so fear creeps in and stops us from moving forward.

Do you know what "Atychiphobia" is? It is an intense, irrational fear of making mistakes, failing, or not meeting expectations, often to the point where it can prevent individuals from pursuing goals, trying new things, or taking risks. This phobia can significantly impact one's personal and professional life, as the fear can lead to procrastination, avoidance, or self-sabotage. How do you know you are afraid of failing? If you can say yes to any of these—ding ding—this is a problem for you:

- Do you procrastinate a lot on your goals and find ways to self-sabotage?
- Do you struggle with low self-esteem and are always telling yourself you are not good enough?
- Do you only do things you know you are good at and can do successfully?
- Do you avoid challenging yourself to step out of your comfort zone?
- Are you reluctant to try new things?
- Do you worry a lot about what other people think?
- Do you tend to tell people beforehand that you won't succeed so they lower their expectations?

Here is why you must deal with this fear of failure: you will struggle to set bigger goals or dream bigger for yourself.

You can accomplish many things in life in your comfort zone, but a blessed and abundant life is not found in your comfort zone. God is calling you for more. I wish I could say there is just one thing you can do and fear will vanish, but I can't.

I feel fear so many times on my faith walk. I used to hear that the antidote for fear is faith—to believe in yourself. While I do believe having faith is helpful in dealing with fear sometimes, I believe the biblical approach to fear is to accept God's perfect love.

"There is no fear in love. But perfect love drives out fear, because fear has to do with punishment. The one who fears is not made perfect in love." (1 John 4:18 – NIV).

We fear because we lack trust in something, mostly ourselves. But what if we take our eyes off ourselves—or anyone else—and gaze on our Father?

"So do not fear, for I am with you; do not be dismayed, for I am your God. I will strengthen you and help you; I will uphold you with my righteous right hand." (Isaiah 41:10 – NIV).

God has a plan for our lives, and He often challenges us to step out in faith and do something beyond our control and

131

comfort zone. The best way to really overcome fear is to trust God's heart towards you and believe in His perfect love. Choose to believe that no matter what happens—including failing at something—He can use it for His glory.

Instead of fearing failure, fear God instead. The fear of God is the beginning of wisdom (see Proverbs 9:10). If you fear God, you will be obedient and desire to be in His will.

Fear is a part of life. Failure is a part of life.

You must choose to not allow the fear of failure to hinder your blessings. Go after everything God has in store for you, and if you happen to fail along the way, remember it is a learning process for you, so get up and do better next time.

Self-Check Prompts

If you do fail, do you think you will recover?

_____

_____

_____

_____

_____

Ask yourself, *"Is this something God is leading me to do?"* Knowing does not always guarantee success, but knowing you are being obedient will build confidence, even if there is a risk of failure.

_____

_____

_____

_____

_____

Have you prayed about the fear of failing? Take a moment to write out a prayer asking God to help you find peace and see clearly any actions you need to take toward your goals.

_____

_____

_____

_____

If you knew that failure was not an option, what would you start doing right now?

_____

_____

_____

_____

"Failure is not the opposite of success; it is a prerequisite for success."
—Crystal Daye

Success Strategy #16

Pray Plan Persevere

> *"Be joyful in hope, patient in affliction, faithful in prayer."*
> *(Romans 12:12 – NIV).*

Power Keys

- Persistent prayer and Spirit-led planning motivates and equips us to live purposefully and abundantly.
- More prayer, more power; little prayer, little power; no prayer, no power.
- Confidence comes from pursuing your passion and persevering in your purpose.

Throughout your journey of purpose and faith, you will experience obstacles. You will be challenged, your faith tested, and you will face opposition. As a result, you need to PRAY, PLAN, and PERSEVERE.

If I had to share all the opposition and obstacles I have faced over the years, I don't know when I would stop writing. My desire to obey God, live purposefully, achieve my dreams, and leave a godly legacy keeps me motivated and not allow disappointments to cause me to give up on the abundant life God promised me.

Pray Without Ceasing

We see moral values in our society declining, with people encouraging us to live life without God. Don't fall for that trap! Prayer is one of the most powerful tools God—the Creator and Life Giver—has given us to commune with Him, help us make better choices, and grow in faith to please Him.

Developing a consistent prayer life will help you be more resilient when life's challenges throw you off course. Practice journaling prayer requests and interceding for others, lay your desires and dreams before God, cast your cares on Him, and seek His direction and wisdom in every decision.

"Very early in the morning, while it was still dark, Jesus got up, left the house and went off to a solitary place, where he prayed." (Mark 1:35 – NIV).

Develop Various Life Plans

You can choose to live your life by accident or by purpose. Choosing to live by purpose means you have dreams, visualize possibilities, set goals, and commit to working towards your future endeavors. You need to have various life plans, such as a wealth plan, vacation plans, personal development goals, health plans, etc. Planning helps you to be more confident because you have a vision for what you want. It enhances your focus and diminishes distractions. It gives you a greater sense of purpose, balance, peace, and passion.

We know that God ultimately has all control, and we don't know what tomorrow may bring. But making plans is a way we build and demonstrate our faith in God.

"The plans of the diligent lead surely to abundance, but everyone who is hasty comes only to poverty." (Proverbs 21:5 – ESV).

Persevere in Faith

To persevere means to maintain purpose in spite of difficulty or discouragement.

"When the world says, "Give up," hope whispers, "Try it one more time."
—Unknown

137

Perseverance means you are committed to your goals; this will increase your confidence, give you the courage to face your fears and decrease self-doubt. If you persevere, you will achieve your true potential. Remember, you can do anything you set your mind to because Christ has given you the strength.

"And let us not grow weary of doing good, for in due season we will reap, if we do not give up.." (Galatians 6:9 - ESV).

Self-Check Prompts

Write out a prayer of praise for all God has accomplished in your life.

_____

_____

_____

_____

_____

What are you most grateful for?

_____

_____

_____

_____

_____

How can you improve your prayer life?

_____

_____

_____

_____

_____

How will you ensure you keep going, even if you face obstacles in life?

_____

_____

_____

_____

_____

"Does it make sense to pray for guidance about the future if we are not obeying in the thing that lies before us today? How many momentous events in scripture depended on one person's seemingly small act of obedience? Rest assured: Do what God tells you to do now, and depend upon it, and you will be shown what to do next."
— *Elisabeth Elliot*

Conclusion

It took me four years to bring this book to life. I wrote the chapters, contemplated several titles, and almost threw in the towel, thinking this wasn't a "good" book because it wasn't coming together.

But I am grateful this is the season, in God's perfect timing, for it to finally come together, and it is even more impactful now because I finally realized that to be *Divinely Blessed* is for such a time as this.

What does it mean to be divinely blessed? It means walking in the fullness of God's promises for your life. It means knowing deep in your heart that you are favored, chosen, and set apart for a greater purpose.

This book was written with practical, personal empowerment success strategies that have helped me understand what true abundance really is.

As Ambitious Jesus Girls, we often face the challenge of balancing our ambitions with the calling to live a life that glorifies God. But here's the beauty: God's plan for your life is abundant. He has placed gifts, talents, and desires within you, not for them to be hidden but for them to shine and make an impact in this world.

Here's the truth: our scarcity mindset is often the greatest hindrance to living the divinely blessed life God has intended for us. A scarcity mindset tells you there is not enough—whether that is money, opportunities, or even worth. It whispers, *"Maybe God's blessings aren't for you"* or *"What if you fail?"* This mindset is rooted in fear and can block the abundant life God desires for you.

Overcoming this mindset starts with recognizing that you are not limited by what you see in the natural world. God is a God of abundance. When you shift your thinking from scarcity to abundance, you begin to live in expectation of God's favor, and you know He has more than enough resources, wisdom, and opportunities to fulfill His purpose in your life.

Being divinely blessed doesn't mean life will be without challenges. Instead, it means that amid those trials, you can stand firm, knowing God will never leave or forsake you. It means trusting that His plans for you are greater than you can imagine and that as you step out in faith—whether in your career, ministry, business, or personal life—God has already paved the way for your success.

Know that you are equipped for the calling God has placed on your heart. You don't have to wait for permission to pursue greatness because you are DIVINELY BLESSED.

About The Author

Crystal Daye is an award-winning author, International Speaker, Corporate Trainer, and Global Book and Sales Coach.

She has combined her strong business acumen to become a sought-after expert in personal branding, digital marketing, book publishing and book monetization. As the CEO of DayeLight Publishers, she helps new and emerging authors write, publish, market, and monetize their books so they can advance their business and career goals.

As a woman of faith, Crystal believes in servant leadership, and she unselfishly uses the platforms God has given her to positively influence and impact lives globally. She is the host of the award-winning DayeLight Show aired on MTM TV and also the visionary behind the Reach Millions Author Live and Kingdom Indie Author Award (the largest annual faith-based author conference and book fair and author awards in the Caribbean).

Crystal has been featured on numerous local and international platforms, podcasts, and publications, including being named as a Yahoo Finance Top Book Coach. She enjoys traveling, reading, cooking, and spending time with her beautiful daughte.r Christelle.

To connect with Crystal, visit her website at www.crystaldaye.com or www.dayelightpublishers.com and follow her on IG, FB, and LinkedIn.

For booking, contact crystaldaye@gmail.com